HOW TC

FOR BEGINNERS

A Comprehensive Guide to Mastering Baseball from Rules Scoring Strategies, Instructions, And More

Larry D. Browne

COPYRIGHT PAGE

Table of Contents

Introduction

Baseball, often referred to as "America's pastime," is more than just a sport—it's a cultural phenomenon that has captured the hearts of millions worldwide. This introductory section aims to explore the unique qualities that make baseball a beloved and enduring game.

Why Baseball?

Why, indeed, choose baseball? As we explore the tapestry of this beloved sport, we find reasons that extend far beyond the diamond. Baseball is more than a game; it's a narrative, a cultural phenomenon that has left an indelible mark on the hearts of millions.

The Tapestry of History: Baseball's roots stretch deep into history, evolving over decades and weaving itself into the fabric of nations. From sandlots to stadiums, understanding the historical context of the game enriches our appreciation for its enduring appeal.

A Game of Strategy and Skill: Baseball is a cerebral dance, a strategic contest between pitcher and batter, manager and opponent. Uncover the layers of skill that make this game both an art and a science, where split-second decisions shape the course of play.

Community and Tradition: Beyond the game itself, baseball is a communal experience, fostering connections that bridge generations. From fathers teaching sons to the camaraderie of cheering on a team, the sense of tradition and belonging is woven into the very essence of baseball.

Who Can Play?

The beauty of baseball lies in its inclusivity—it's a sport for everyone, regardless of age, gender, or skill level. This section is an ode to the diversity that makes baseball a tapestry of shared experiences.

For the Young and Young at Heart: Children grasp a glove for the first time, and seasoned players step up to the plate with equal enthusiasm. Baseball is a lifelong journey, inviting players of all ages to find joy in its nuances.

Fostering Youth Development: Explore the benefits of introducing children to baseball, from cultivating physical fitness to instilling values of teamwork and discipline. Through youth engagement, we sow the seeds for lifelong passion and a deep appreciation for the game.

A Game for All: Baseball's embrace extends beyond stereotypes and welcomes players of all backgrounds. Whether you're a seasoned athlete or a newcomer, there's a place for you on the diamond. Discover the stories of individuals who found their love for the game, breaking barriers and challenging expectations.

The Joy of Baseball

At its core, baseball is an orchestra of joy—each swing, pitch, and catch resonates with the thrill of competition and the shared delight of a community brought together by a common love.

Moments of Elation: Few experiences match the exhilaration of hitting a home run, making a stellar catch, or witnessing a perfect pitch. These moments of pure joy are the building blocks of a baseball player's journey.

Camaraderie and Connection: Baseball is more than a game; it's a shared experience that fosters connections and builds friendships. From the dugout to the stands, the sense of camaraderie is as integral to the sport as the leather of a well-worn glove.

A Love Passed Down: Generations bond over baseball, passing down stories, traditions, and a love for the game. Through the joy it brings, baseball becomes a timeless thread that connects families and communities.

As we embark on this exploration of baseball for beginners, let the pages that follow be a guide to the intricacies, the stories, and the pure joy that defines this remarkable sport. Whether you're stepping onto the field for the first time or cheering from the stands, welcome to the world of baseball—a world where the crack of the bat and the roar of the crowd create a symphony of memories that last a lifetime.

CHAPTER 1

Understanding the Basics

Welcome to the core essentials of baseball—an exploration of the fundamental elements that shape the game. In this section, we dive into the very essence of baseball, from the structure of the game to the rules governing it, the roles each player plays, and the equipment that makes it all possible.

Overview of the Game

At its heart, baseball is a symphony of strategy, athleticism, and anticipation. Let's take a closer look at the key components that define the flow of the game.

Innings and Outs: Baseball unfolds inning by inning, with each team taking turns at bat and in the field. An inning consists of both offensive and defensive halves, and the objective is to score runs while preventing the opposing team from doing the same. Understanding the concept of outs is pivotal, as each team has three outs to work with before switching roles.

Scoring Runs: The primary goal in baseball is to score runs by successfully navigating around the bases. A player scores a run by reaching home plate after touching first, second, and third bases in sequence. The intricate dance of base running and defensive plays adds layers of excitement to the game.

Pitching and Hitting: The dynamic interplay between pitcher and batter is a central focus. The pitcher aims to throw strikes within the designated strike zone, while the batter endeavors to connect with the pitched ball, sending it into play.

Rules and Regulations

For the uninitiated, baseball's rules may seem intricate, but they form the backbone of the game. Let's unravel the essential regulations that govern play on the diamond.

Fair and Foul Territory: The playing field is divided into fair and foul territory. Hits landing in fair territory contribute to the game, while those landing in foul territory are considered out of play. This distinction plays a crucial role in determining the outcome of each play.

Balls and Strikes: A pitch can be a ball or a strike, depending on its location within the strike zone. The number of balls and strikes influences a batter's fate at the plate, affecting their chances of reaching base or being declared out.

Base Running Rules: As players move around the bases, various rules come into play. Understanding concepts like tagging up, stealing bases, and the dynamics of force plays enhances the appreciation of the strategic intricacies of the game.

Positions and Player Roles

Every player on a baseball field has a designated position and role, contributing to the team's overall strategy and success.

Infield Positions: The infield is manned by players stationed at first base, second base, shortstop, and third base. Each has specific responsibilities, from fielding ground balls to executing double plays.

Outfield Positions: Outfielders patrol the outer edges of the field, with positions in left field, center field, and right field. Their primary duties include catching fly balls, preventing extra-base hits, and making accurate throws.

Battery (Pitcher and Catcher): The pitcher and catcher form a crucial partnership known as the battery. The pitcher delivers pitches with precision, while the catcher receives and strategizes, guiding the team through the game.

Equipment Overview

To play baseball effectively, players require specific equipment. Understanding the tools of the trade is essential for both newcomers and seasoned players.

Bats: Bats come in various sizes and materials. Choosing the right bat is crucial for a player's comfort and performance. Regulations also dictate the specifications for legal bats.

Balls: Baseballs are carefully constructed with specific materials and stitching patterns.

The condition of the ball can influence its trajectory and play, making it an essential element of the game.

Gloves and Mitts: Different positions require different types of gloves. Fielders use gloves with varying sizes and designs to suit their roles, while catchers employ mitts specially designed to catch pitched balls.

Protective Gear: Helmets are mandatory for batters and recommended for base runners. Catchers wear additional protective gear, including shin guards and chest protectors, to guard against potential injuries.

Understanding these basics lays the foundation for a deeper appreciation of baseball. As we delve further into the intricacies of the sport, each element will come alive, contributing to the rich tapestry that is the game of baseball.

CHAPTER 2

Getting Started

Embarking on your baseball journey is an exciting venture filled with possibilities. In this section, we guide you through the initial steps of getting started—from finding the right team or league to selecting the essential gear and understanding the basic field etiquette.

Finding Your Local Team or League

Joining a local team or league is a fantastic way to immerse yourself in the world of baseball and build lasting connections within your community.

Community Resources: Start by exploring community resources, such as local sports clubs, community centers, or school programs. These often serve as hubs for baseball activities and can provide information about nearby teams or leagues.

Online Platforms: Utilize online platforms and websites dedicated to local sports and recreation. Many communities have websites or social media groups where teams and leagues post updates, announcements, and registration details.

Ask Around: Don't hesitate to ask friends, family, or colleagues if they know of any local baseball opportunities. Word of mouth can lead to valuable insights and recommendations.

Youth Programs: If you're a parent or guardian looking to involve your child in baseball, schools and youth programs are excellent starting points. These programs often cater to different age groups and skill levels, providing a supportive environment for beginners.

Choosing the Right Gear

Selecting the right gear is essential for comfort, safety, and optimal performance on the field.

Whether you're a player or a parent preparing a young athlete, here's a guide to the basic gear you'll need.

Baseball Glove: A well-fitted glove is a player's most crucial tool. Choose a glove that matches your position—outfielders, infielders, and catchers each have specialized glove designs.

Baseball Bat: When selecting a bat, consider factors such as length, weight, and material. The right bat should feel comfortable and suit your style of play. Check with league regulations to ensure your bat meets their specifications.

Helmet: Safety is paramount in baseball. A helmet protects the head during batting and base running. Ensure the helmet fits securely and meets safety standards.

Cleats: Baseball cleats provide traction on the field, aiding in quick movements. Look for cleats designed for baseball, with molded or metal spikes, depending on your league's regulations.

Protective Gear: If you're a catcher, invest in additional

protective gear, including shin guards, a chest protector, and a catcher's mask. This equipment safeguards against potential injuries while behind the plate.

Basic Field Etiquette

Understanding and adhering to basic field etiquette is not only a sign of respect but also ensures a positive experience for everyone involved.

Arrive on Time: Punctuality is crucial. Arrive on time for practices, games, and team events. Being prompt shows commitment to the team and allows everyone to make the most of the scheduled time.

Listen to Coaches: Coaches play a vital role in your development as a player. Pay attention to their instructions, ask questions when needed, and implement the feedback they provide.

Respect Teammates and Opponents: Treat your teammates and opponents with respect. Baseball is a team sport, and camaraderie enhances the overall experience for everyone involved.

Maintain the Field: Whether practicing or playing, contribute to the upkeep of the field. Pick up equipment, dispose of trash responsibly, and leave the field in the condition you found it.

Encourage Sportsmanship: Baseball is a game of highs and lows. Embrace the victories with humility and learn from the challenges. Displaying good sportsmanship fosters a positive environment for everyone.

Getting started in baseball is an exhilarating endeavor, and these initial steps pave the way for a fulfilling and enjoyable experience on the diamond. As you step onto the field, remember that each swing, catch, and play is an opportunity to learn, grow, and, most importantly, have fun.

CHAPTER 3

Essential Skills for Beginners

As you begin your baseball journey, mastering fundamental skills is crucial to enjoying the game and contributing to your team's success. In this section, we'll delve into the essential skills

every beginner should focus on—
from the art of throwing and
catching to developing a solid
batting stance and swing,
understanding the fundamentals
of base running, and grasping
basic pitching mechanics.

Throwing and Catching Techniques

Throwing:

Grip: Hold the ball across the seams with your fingertips, creating a backspin for a more accurate throw.

Footwork: Position your feet shoulder-width apart, leading with your non-throwing foot. This helps generate power and accuracy.

Follow Through: Follow through with your throw, pointing your throwing arm toward your target. This ensures a smooth and accurate release.

Catching:

Ready Position: Keep your knees slightly bent, weight on the balls of your feet, and hands positioned in front of you. Stay agile and ready to react.

Eye on the Ball: Focus on the ball from the pitcher's hand to your glove. Tracking the ball helps improve catching accuracy.

Soft Hands: Receive the ball with "soft hands," meaning relaxed fingers and wrists. This minimizes the impact and helps secure the catch.

Proper Batting Stance and Swing

Batting Stance:

Feet Position: Stand with your feet shoulder-width apart and parallel to the pitcher's mound.

Grip: Hold the bat with both hands close together, knuckles aligned, and the bat resting on your back shoulder.

Balance: Distribute your weight evenly on both legs, slightly bending your knees for flexibility and balance.

Swing:

Load: As the pitcher begins the wind-up, shift your weight to your back foot, loading up your swing.

Stride: Take a controlled step forward with your front foot as the pitcher releases the ball, maintaining balance.

Contact: Rotate your hips and shoulders, bringing the bat to meet the ball. Aim for the "sweet spot" on the bat for optimal contact.

Follow Through: Complete your swing with a full follow-through, rotating your hips and shoulders. This motion maximizes power and control.

Base Running Fundamentals

Sprinting Techniques:

Quick Start: Explode off the base with a quick first step.

Turns: When rounding bases, take wide turns to maintain momentum and speed.

Head Up: Keep your head up while running to maintain awareness of the ball's location and potential plays.

Stealing Bases:

Timing: Pay attention to the pitcher's movements to time your steal attempt.

Slide Techniques: Practice proper sliding techniques—feet first or head first—depending on the situation and distance to the base.

4.4 Basic Pitching Mechanics

Wind-Up:

Stance: Stand with your feet shoulder-width apart and perpendicular to the pitching rubber.

Grip: Hold the ball with your fingers across the seams, finding a comfortable grip that allows for control and accuracy.

Delivery:

Step and Stride: Take a controlled step forward with your non-throwing foot and follow with a longer stride toward home plate.

Rotation: Rotate your hips and shoulders, bringing the ball forward in a smooth and controlled motion.

Release: Release the ball with a snapping motion of your wrist, aiming for your target with accuracy.

Follow Through:

Balance: Finish your pitch with a balanced stance, ready to field any potential hits.

Fielding Position: Be prepared to field your position, anticipating a hit back to the mound.

CHAPTER 4

The Game in Action

As the players take the field, the game of baseball comes alive with a rhythm of innings, a symphony of scoring, and the watchful eyes of umpires shaping the narrative. In this section, we explore the dynamic flow of the game in action—from the breakdown of innings to the intricacies of scoring and statistics, and the crucial role of umpires in making decisive calls.

Inning Breakdown

The Ebb and Flow:

Top and Bottom: Each inning is split into two halves—the top and bottom. The visiting team takes its turn at bat in the top half, while the home team defends. Roles reverse in the bottom half.

Three Outs: Both teams strive to accumulate runs while on offense. However, their offensive inning concludes when they incur three outs—whether through strikeouts, catches, or defensive plays.

Switching Sides: After the third out, the teams switch between playing offense and defense. This rotation continues until each team has had its fair share of opportunities in nine innings.

Strategic Maneuvers:

Pitching Changes: Coaches strategically substitute pitchers to gain advantages, adapting to the strengths and weaknesses of the opposing batters.

Defensive Adjustments: Teams may shift their defensive positions based on the tendencies of the hitters, aiming to thwart potential hits.

Scoring and Statistics

Putting Runs on the Board:

Home Runs: The pinnacle of offensive achievement occurs when a batter hits the ball beyond the outfield walls, resulting in a home run. Runs scored by teammates on base also contribute to the tally.

RBIs (Runs Batted In): Batters earn RBIs when their hits enable base runners to successfully cross home plate.

Key Metrics and Numbers:

Batting Average (BA): A player's batting average is calculated by dividing the number of hits by the total number of at-bats. It serves as a gauge of a player's hitting prowess.

Earned Run Average (ERA): A pitcher's ERA is computed by determining the average number of earned runs they allow per nine innings, offering insight into their effectiveness.

Fielding Percentage: Fielding percentage measures a player's defensive proficiency, representing the ratio of successful defensive plays to the total number of opportunities.

Umpires and Their Decisions

Guardians of Fair Play:

Home Plate Umpire: Positioned behind the catcher, the home plate umpire governs the strike zone, calls balls and strikes, and adjudicates plays at home plate.

Base Umpires: Umpires stationed at first, second, and third bases oversee plays involving runners, ensuring adherence to the rules.

Decisive Calls:

Balls and Strikes: Umpires make instantaneous decisions on whether a pitched ball is within the defined strike zone, shaping the flow of the at-bat.

Fair or Foul: Umpires determine the trajectory of hit balls, classifying them as fair or foul based on their landing positions.

Safe or Out: Umpires render verdicts on plays involving runners and fielders, crucially deciding if a runner is safe or out.

The Role of Instant Replay:

Challenges: In certain leagues, managers can challenge umpire decisions, leading to the utilization of instant replay for more accurate outcomes.

Reviewable Plays: Common reviewable scenarios include calls on home runs, fair or foul hits, and close plays at the bases.

CHAPTER 5

Team Dynamics

The essence of baseball lies not just in individual performances but in the synergy of the team. In this section, we explore the vital aspects of team dynamics—from building chemistry among players to effective communication on the field and the development of strategy, especially tailored for beginners.

Building Team Chemistry

Fostering Unity:

Team-Building Activities: Engage in off-field activities that promote camaraderie and teamwork. From bonding exercises to team outings, building connections off the field enhances trust and cooperation on the field.

Support System: Encourage an environment where players support one another. Celebrate successes, lift each other up during challenges, and create a positive atmosphere where everyone feels valued.

Inclusive Culture: Embrace diversity within the team. Recognize and appreciate the unique strengths each player brings to the game, fostering a sense of inclusivity and belonging.

Communication on the Field

Clear and Concise Communication:

Verbal and Non-Verbal Signals: Establish clear signals for communication on the field. Whether it's calling for a fly ball or signaling plays, effective communication ensures everyone is on the same page.

Encourage Open Communication: Create an atmosphere where players feel comfortable expressing ideas and concerns. Encourage open dialogue during practices and games to enhance understanding and teamwork.

Position-Specific Communication: Different positions require specific communication. Infielders need to communicate effectively on who covers which base, while outfielders should coordinate on fly balls to avoid collisions.

Team Strategy for Beginners

Foundational Strategies:

Understanding Roles: Ensure that every player understands their role on the team. Define positions clearly and discuss the responsibilities associated with each.

Basic Offensive Plays: Introduce fundamental offensive plays such as hit and run, bunting, and stealing bases. Understanding these plays lays the groundwork for more advanced strategies.

Defensive Formations: Teach basic defensive formations,

emphasizing the importance of player positioning. Understanding where to stand in different situations enhances defensive efficiency.

Adaptability and Learning:

Adapt to Opponents: Encourage adaptability by discussing strategies to counter different types of opponents. Understanding the strengths and weaknesses of opposing teams can inform game-time decisions.

Continuous Learning: Emphasize a culture of continuous learning. Discuss game outcomes, evaluate performances, and use every experience as an opportunity for improvement.

Encourage Initiative: Foster a sense of initiative among players. Encourage them to think strategically, make decisions on the field, and learn from both successes and challenges.

As you navigate the complexities of team dynamics, remember that every player contributes to the collective story of the team. Through building chemistry, fostering clear communication, and introducing strategic elements, your team can evolve into a cohesive unit, creating a memorable and enjoyable baseball experience for everyone involved.

CHAPTER 6

Common Mistakes and How to Avoid Them

In the world of baseball, mistakes are inevitable, especially for beginners. The key is not to dwell on them but to use each misstep as an opportunity for growth. In this section, we'll explore common rookie errors and provide insights on learning from them. Additionally, we'll offer tips for improving quickly, helping you navigate the learning curve of this intricate sport.

Rookie Errors and How to Learn from Them

*1. Overthinking at the Plate:

Error: Swinging at every pitch without a plan or overthinking each at-bat.

Learning Opportunity: Develop a batting approach. Understand the strike zone, be patient, and look for pitches you can drive.

*2. Neglecting Defensive Fundamentals:

Error: Forgetting the basics of fielding, such as proper stance, ready position, and anticipation.

Learning Opportunity: Focus on the fundamentals during practice. Regularly practice ground balls, pop flies, and throwing to improve defensive skills.

*3. Misjudging Fly Balls in the Outfield:

Error: Misjudging the trajectory of fly balls, leading to missed catches or errors.

Learning Opportunity: Work on tracking fly balls during practice. Pay attention to the flight of the ball and practice catching routine fly balls from different angles.

*4. Ignoring Base Running Fundamentals:

Error: Making mistakes on the base paths, such as not tagging up, missing signs, or hesitating.

Learning Opportunity: Study base running rules and practice scenarios during drills. Understand the importance of proper leads and when to steal or stay put.

*5. Poor Pitching Mechanics:

Error: Inconsistent pitching mechanics leading to wild pitches, lack of accuracy, or fatigue.

Learning Opportunity: Work with coaches to refine pitching mechanics. Regularly practice pitching drills to improve control and stamina.

*6.   Neglecting   Physical Conditioning:

Error: Underestimating the physical demands of the game and neglecting overall fitness.

Learning Opportunity: Prioritize strength and conditioning. Develop cardiovascular endurance, agility, and flexibility to enhance overall performance.

7.2 Tips for Improving Quickly

*1. Consistent Practice:

Tip: Regular, focused practice is key to improvement.

Action: Dedicate time to daily or weekly practice sessions. Focus on specific skills, and gradually increase the intensity of your drills.

*2. Seek Feedback:

Tip: Actively seek feedback from coaches and experienced players.

Action: Ask for constructive criticism after practices or games. Use feedback to identify areas for improvement and set specific goals.

*3. Watch and Learn:

Tip: Learn from watching experienced players and professional games.

Action: Analyze games, study player techniques, and observe strategic decisions. Apply what you learn to your own practice and gameplay.

*4. Mental Preparation:

Tip: Develop mental resilience and focus.

Action: Practice mindfulness techniques, visualize success, and cultivate a positive mindset. Mental preparation is as crucial as physical training.

*5. Specialized Training:

Tip: Consider specialized training in areas where you need improvement.

Action: Attend clinics or workshops focused on specific skills. Seek guidance from specialized coaches to address weaknesses.

*6. Set Attainable Goals:

Tip: Break down your improvement into achievable goals.

Action: Set short-term and long-term goals. Celebrate small victories along the way, and use setbacks as motivation to keep pushing forward.

CHAPTER 7

Staying Safe and Healthy

Ensuring the well-being of players is paramount in the world of baseball. In this section, we'll delve into essential practices to stay safe and healthy on the field, covering warm-up and cool-down exercises to prevent injuries and providing tips for injury prevention.

Warm-up and Cool-down Exercises

Warm-Up Exercises:

Purpose: The warm-up is crucial to prepare your body for the physical demands of baseball, increasing blood flow to muscles and enhancing flexibility.

Routine:

Dynamic Stretching: Incorporate dynamic stretches such as leg swings, arm circles, and torso twists to improve joint mobility.

Light Cardio: Engage in light jogging or skipping to elevate your heart rate gradually.

Sport-Specific Drills: Include drills that mimic baseball movements, such as light throwing, catching, and hitting.

Cool-Down Exercises:

Purpose: The cool-down is essential for aiding muscle

recovery, preventing stiffness, and reducing the risk of injury after intense physical activity.

Routine:

Static Stretching: Focus on static stretches for major muscle groups, holding each stretch for 15-30 seconds to improve flexibility.

Foam Rolling: Use a foam roller to release tension in muscles, promoting recovery and preventing tightness.

Hydration: Conclude with adequate hydration to replenish fluids lost during play.

Injury Prevention Tips

Strength and Conditioning:

Tip: Build overall strength and conditioning to withstand the physical demands of the game.

Action: Incorporate a well-rounded fitness routine, including strength training, cardiovascular exercises, and agility drills. A strong and conditioned body is less prone to injuries.

Proper Technique:

Tip: Emphasize proper technique in all aspects of the game.

Action: Work closely with coaches to ensure that you are using the correct form in throwing, hitting, and fielding. Proper technique reduces the risk of strain on muscles and joints.

Rest and Recovery:

Tip: Prioritize sufficient rest and recovery between practices and games.

Action: Adequate sleep, rest days, and proper nutrition are essential for optimal recovery. Listen to your body and allow it the time it needs to recover.

Hydration:

Tip: Maintain proper hydration levels before, during, and after playing.

Action: Drink water consistently throughout the day, especially in warmer weather. Dehydration can lead to fatigue and increase the risk of muscle cramps.

Proper Equipment:

Tip: Use well-fitted and appropriate equipment for your position and the game.

Action: Ensure your glove, bat, helmet, and other gear are in good condition and suit your size and playing style. A proper-fitting helmet, for example, is crucial for head protection.

Listen to Your Body:

Tip: Pay attention to any signs of discomfort or pain.

Action: If you experience persistent pain or discomfort, seek medical advice promptly.

Ignoring minor issues can lead to more severe injuries.

Cross-Training:

Tip: Engage in cross-training activities to promote overall fitness.

Action: Include activities such as swimming, cycling, or yoga to enhance flexibility, strength, and balance. Cross-training can reduce the risk of overuse injuries.

**8. Pre-Season Physicals:

Tip: Undergo pre-season physical examinations.

Action: Regular check-ups with healthcare professionals can identify any underlying health issues and ensure you are fit to participate in physical activities.

By integrating these warm-up and cool-down routines, following injury prevention tips, and maintaining a holistic approach to health, you'll create a foundation for a safe and enjoyable experience on the baseball field. Prioritizing your well-being not only enhances your performance but also ensures longevity and fulfillment in the sport.

CHAPTER 8

Beyond the Basics

As your understanding of baseball grows, it's time to explore additional dimensions of the sport. This section delves into different baseball formats, opportunities for advancement, and the crucial aspects of baseball etiquette and sportsmanship.

Exploring Different Baseball Formats (e.g., Softball)

Softball:

Introduction: Softball is a variant of baseball with some key differences, such as a smaller field, a larger and softer ball, and underhand pitching. It's a popular alternative, often played recreationally and competitively.

Format: Softball is played in various formats, including slow-pitch and fast-pitch. Each has its own set of rules and nuances, offering diverse experiences for players.

Strategy Differences: The smaller field in softball often leads to faster-paced games, requiring quick reflexes and strategic play. The transition from baseball to softball or vice versa can provide a fresh perspective on the sport.

Opportunities for Advancement

Competitive Leagues:

Local Leagues: Joining local leagues allows for regular, organized gameplay. These leagues often cater to different skill levels, providing opportunities for both beginners and experienced players.

Travel Teams: As skills develop, consider trying out for travel teams that compete at regional or national levels. Travel teams often attract college scouts, opening doors for advancement in the sport.

High School and College Baseball:

High School Teams: Representing your high school team provides exposure and the chance to compete at a more competitive level. High school baseball also serves as a stepping stone for college recruitment.

College Scholarships: Exceptional players may have the opportunity to earn college scholarships, combining academics with their passion for baseball. College baseball programs offer a higher level of competition and exposure to scouts.

Professional Baseball:

Minor Leagues: Players with exceptional talent often start in the minor leagues, working their way up to the major leagues. The minor leagues serve as a training ground for emerging talent.

Major Leagues: The pinnacle of the baseball journey is reaching the major leagues. Becoming a professional baseball player requires exceptional skills, dedication, and perseverance.

Baseball Etiquette and Sportsmanship

Respecting Opponents:

Fair Play: Treat opponents with respect, adhering to the principles of fair play. Follow the rules of the game and uphold a sense of integrity on and off the field.

Upholding Team Spirit:

Teamwork: Emphasize the importance of teamwork. Encourage and support your teammates, recognizing that success is a collective effort.

Handling Success and Failure:

Graceful Wins and Losses: Whether celebrating a victory or facing defeat, do so with grace. Acknowledge opponents' efforts and learn from every experience.

Respecting Umpires and Officials:

Umpire Decisions: Umpires play a vital role in the game. Accept their decisions without dispute, understanding that they contribute to the integrity of the sport.

Community Involvement:

Giving Back: Get involved in community initiatives related to baseball. Volunteer, coach younger players, or participate in events that promote the sport within your community.

Inclusivity and Diversity:

Welcoming Environment: Foster an inclusive and diverse environment within the baseball community. Encourage players of all backgrounds to participate and feel welcomed.

Off-Field Conduct:

Representing the Sport: Remember that your conduct off the field reflects on the sport as a whole. Uphold high standards of behavior in your personal and public life.

Conclusion

Embarking on the journey of baseball, whether as a beginner or seasoned player, opens the door to a world of excitement, camaraderie, and personal growth. Throughout this comprehensive guide, we've covered the fundamentals and intricacies of the sport, offering a roadmap for your baseball adventure.

From understanding the basics of the game and essential skills for beginners to exploring the nuances of strategy, team dynamics, and staying safe and healthy, each aspect contributes to the holistic experience on the diamond. Whether you're fielding a ground ball, swinging for the fences, or strategizing with your teammates, baseball is a symphony of skill, strategy, and teamwork.

Beyond the diamond, we've ventured into different formats like softball, explored opportunities for advancement, and highlighted the importance of baseball etiquette and sportsmanship. The values cultivated through baseball extend far beyond the game, shaping individuals into resilient, team-oriented, and sportsmanlike contributors to their communities.

As you dive into the world of baseball, remember that every swing, catch, and play is an opportunity for growth and enjoyment. Whether you find yourself on a local little league field, a high school diamond, or dream of stepping onto the grand stage of the major leagues, savor each moment and embrace the lessons the sport offers.

May your baseball journey be filled with thrilling games, lasting friendships, and a love for the timeless beauty of America's pastime. Whether you're a player, coach, or fan, the magic of baseball lies not just in the crack of the bat or the perfect pitch but in the timeless bond shared by those who cherish the game. Play ball!

Made in the USA
Columbia, SC
09 November 2024